A Little Book of
Serenity

A Little Book of
Serenity

Ruskin Bond

SPEAKING
TIGER

SPEAKING TIGER PUBLISHING PVT. LTD
4381/4 Ansari Road, Daryaganj,
New Delhi–110002, India

Anthology copyright © Speaking Tiger 2016
Introduction copyright © Ruskin Bond 2016

ISBN: 978-93-86050-35-9
eISBN: 978-93-86050-33-5

10 9 8 7 6 5 4 3 2 1

Typeset in Garamond Pro by SÜRYA, New Delhi
Printed at Thomson Press India Ltd.

All rights reserved.
No part of this publication may be reproduced,
transmitted, or stored in a retrieval system,
in any form or by any means, electronic,
mechanical, photocopying, recording
or otherwise, without the prior
permission of the publisher.

This book is sold subject to the condition that it
shall not, by way of trade or otherwise, be lent,
resold, hired out, or otherwise circulated,
without the publisher's prior consent,
in any form of binding or cover other
than that in which it is published.

Introduction

Some years ago, on a busy road outside a railway station, I saw a yogi lying on a bed of nails. He was taking a quiet nap, and when he got up he looked very rested, very serene.

I suppose that's one form of serenity—looking comfortable where others would find discomfort.

My Uncle Ken, the laziest man in the world, proclaimed that he could do the same thing. He got a thick mattress, placed it over the bed of nails, spread himself out upon it, and gave us a self-satisfied grin. I suppose that too was a serenity of a sort. Or was it serendipity?

In this workaday, competitive, computerized world I find it very hard to find people who are truly serene. As people rush around in their cars, or on their bikes, they are usually snarling at each other, anxious to overtake, to get ahead. Nervous tension oozes from their pores. Serenity is just a word they have heard of somewhere.

Or sit in front of your TV set any evening. Tune in to the news channels. And what will you find?

Angry citizens, agitated politicians, excitable TV anchors, sermonizing holy men, opinionated celebrities… Serenity is rarely to be seen.

Perhaps you will find it only in the cradle. I remember an African mother crooning a lullaby to her sleeping infant: 'How can there be a baby with no crying? How can there be a story with no ending?' And she answers her own questions: 'A baby when it's sleeping has no crying. A story of "I love you" has no ending…'

A sleeping baby, a tender lullaby, and peace spread all over that loving face. It happens sometimes.

I have seen serenity in the faces of old people, those who have come to terms with life and the knowledge that life on earth is not permanent. An old lady contemplating a rose, an old man dreaming of other days, or gazing at the distant mountains and wondering at *their* serenity; for the serenity of nature is the serenity of perfection. Sometimes I think that serenity can only be acquired through humility. Receive failure and defeat with a smile. You will make more friends that way. And when you run your race again, that smile, your serene and loving nature, will take you further than all the fast cars in the world.

.Ruskin Bond.

There is no harm in sitting
 in an office and making money,
but sometimes you must look out of the
    window. And look at the changing light.

Th e old pond,
A frog jumps in:
Plop!
—*Matsuo Basho (tr. Alan Watts)*

Lord, give me a quiet mind,
Th at I might listen;
A gentle tone of voice,
Th at I might comfort others;
A sound and healthy body,
Th at I might share
In the joy of walking
And leaping and running;
And a good sense of direction
So I might know just
where I'm going!

'all morning
clouds climb up the valley;
my tea-kettle whistles.'
—*Guru T. Ladakhi*

❧

'With no bird singing
Th e mountain is yet more still.'
—*Zen saying*

❧

'If you want inner peace find it
in solitude, not speed,
and if you would find yourself,
look to the land from which you
came and to which you go.'
—*Stewart Udall*

'There's more to life than
increasing its speed.'
—*Mahatma Gandhi*

'Old friends pass away, new friends appear. It is just like the days. An old day passes, a new day arrives. Th e important thing is to make it meaningful: a meaningful friend—or a meaningful day.'
—*Dalai Lama*

An outbreak of spring:
The sun comes up and the
walls of the houses are suddenly
patched with splashes of colour;
and just as suddenly the trees
seem to have burst into flower;
for in the forest are armies of
rhododendrons, poinsettias
dance by the river;
the snows in the mountains
have melted and the streams are
rushing torrents;
the young grass holds both dew
and sun,
and makes an emerald of every
dewdrop.

'I have books, work, a garden;
I have the children and the
dogs and,
when I feel I am getting
infantile,
I have the books again.'
—*Rumer Godden*

'Love your art, poor as it may be,
which thou hast learned, and be
content with it; and pass through
the rest of life making thyself
neither the tyrant nor the slave
of any man.'
—*Marcus Aurelius*

.18.

.Ruskin Bond.

.A Little Book of Serenity.

.20.

.Ruskin Bond.

Since my house burned down
I now own a better view
of the rising moon.

— Mizuta Masahide

Simple pleasures:
Browsing among old books.
The cooing of doves and pigeons.
Blue jays (rollers) in flight,
indulging in their aerial
acrobatics.
Walking barefoot over dew-
drenched grass.
Peeling an orange.
Listening to street cries—sellers
of balloons, candyfloss, pickles,
gol-guppas.

.Ruskin Bond.

Beer in the sun. High in the
spruce tree the barbet calls,
heralding summer.
A few puffy clouds drift lazily
over the mountains.

'By all means use sometimes
to be alone!
Salute thyself: see what thy soul
doth wear!'
—*George Herbert*

'People forget that their lives
will end soon.
For those who remember,
quarrels come to an end.'
—*The Dhammapada*

'The greatest blessings of
mankind are within us and
within our reach. A wise man is
content with his lot, whatever
it may be, without wishing for
what he has not.'
—*Seneca*

Some compensations of summer:

Shade, and an iced drink.
Laziness.
Siesta.
A cool breeze.
Wearing as few or whatever
clothes as one likes.
The exquisite shock from a
bucket of cold water.
And the fruit, the fruit!

Treated myself to Sir Harry Lauder singing 'Loch Lomond', Dame Clara Buck singing 'Comin' through the Rye', and Arthur Askey singing 'We have no bananas today'. Passers-by stopped, some to listen, others to ask if I couldn't play something better. But everyone seemed to enjoy the diversion.

It's a busy world, I know,
And we must hurry
here and there
And not ask who or why
or where,
For fear our credits fall too low.
But here upon this hilly crest
There's some respite; and when
The fretting day is done,
Beneath the cherry tree
there's rest.

I do not have to climb a mountain peak in order to appreciate the grandeur of this earth. Th ere are wild dandelions flowering on the patch of wasteland just outside my windows. A wild rose bush will come to life in the spring rain, and on summer nights the honeysuckle will send its fragrance through the open windows.

.Ruskin Bond.

Notes

. Ruskin Bond .

.A Little Book of Serenity.

32.

.Ruskin Bond.

Were it not for
the excess of your talking
and the turmoil in your hearts,
you would see what I see
and hear what I hear.

— Ibn al-Arabi

'You've seen the sun flatten and take strange shapes just before it sinks in the ocean. Do you have to tell yourself every time that it's an illusion caused by atmospheric dust and light distorted by the sea, or do you simply enjoy the beauty of it?'
—*John Steinbeck*

The rains set in, and the sun only
makes brief appearances.
The hills turn a lush green.
Ferns spring up on walls and
tree trunks.
Giant lilies rear up like leopards
from the tall grass.
A white mist coils and uncoils as
it floats up from the valley.
Leeches are aplenty; still,
it is beautiful.

The clouds part and the moon appears—a full moon, bathing the mountains in pollen-yellow light. Mussoorie basks in the moonlight, each lighted dwelling a firefly in the night.

'Night with her train of stars' is always enticing. The poet Henley found her so. But he also wrote of 'her great gift of sleep', and it is this gift that I accept with gratitude and humility. For it is good to be up and dancing in the morning dew.

.Ruskin Bond.

The rain stops. The clouds begin to break up, the sun strikes the steep hill on my left. I hear the tinkle of cowbells. And suddenly, clear and pure, the song of the whistling-thrush emerges like a dark sweet secret from the depths of the ravine.

'It is not enough to be busy.
So are the ants.
Th e question is: What are we
busy about?'
—*Th oreau*

❦

'Asked, who is the rich man?
Epictetus replied, "He who is
content."'
—*Epictetus*

❦

This leaf, so complete in itself,
Is only part of the tree.
And this tree,
so complete in itself,
Is only part of the forest.
And the forest runs down from
the hill to the sea,
And the sea,
so complete in itself,
Rests like a raindrop
In the hand of God.

'The Buddhists...put their prayer
flags where the wind
will blow them and their prayer
wheels in the streams
where the water will
turn them and
get on with their work while the
prayers are said.
I think that is wisdom.'
—*Rumer Godden*

.41.

.A Little Book of Serenity.

.42.

.Ruskin Bond.

.43.

.A Little Book of Serenity.

.Ruskin Bond.

I'm all right,
I'm doing my own thing,
And in my own right
I'm a king!

Coming home, I took a shortcut through a forest. A swarm of butterflies drifted across the path. A woodpecker pecked industriously at a tree bark. Overhead, wild duck flew north, all travelling without passports. Birds and butterflies recognize no borders.

I sat in a teashop, tested my teeth on an old bun, and washed it down with milky tea. Th e bun had been around for some time, but so had I, so we were quits.

.Ruskin Bond.

'Either thou livest here and hast already accustomed thyself to it, or thou art going away, and this was thy own will; or thou art dying and hast discharged thy duty. But besides these things there is nothing. Be of good cheer, then.'
—*Marcus Aurelius*

'The morning wind scatters,
The morning wind scatters its
fresh fragrance.
We must get up and
breathe it in,
that wind which lets us live.
Breathe before it's gone.'
—*Rumi*

No moon; the stars just
beginning to appear. A bend
in the road, and a light shining
from a kerosene lamp swinging
outside a small roadside hut.

'Losing too is still ours;
and even forgetting
still has a shape in the kingdom
of transformation.
When something's let go of, it
circles; and though we are
rarely the center
of the circle, it draws around us
its unbroken, marvelous curve.'
—*Rilke (tr. Stephen Mitchell)*

'As I walked out the door toward the gate that would lead to my freedom, I knew if I didn't leave my bitterness and hatred behind, I'd still be in prison.'
—*Nelson Mandela*

'Letting go gives us freedom, and freedom is the only condition for happiness. If, in our heart, we still cling to anything—anger, anxiety, or possessions—we cannot be free.'
—*Th ich Nhat Hanh*

'God, grant me the serenity to
accept the things
I cannot change,
Courage to change
the things I can,
And wisdom to know
the difference.'
—*Reinhold Niebuhr*

.53.

.A Little Book of Serenity.

.Ruskin Bond.

.55.

.A Little Book of Serenity.

. Ruskin Bond .

> Every day no Christmas,
> an' every day no rainy day.

— A West Indian proverb

Life has its ups and downs,
but now and then it springs a
surprise, such as an encounter
with an old friend, and makes us
want to go on a little longer.

'Pale moon,
A riverside bar;
Th e company of a childhood
friend.'
—*Anonymous*

Th ere is a brook at the bottom of the hill. From where I live I can always hear its murmur, but I am no longer conscious of the sound except when I return from a trip to the plains. And yet I am so used to its constant music that when I leave it behind I feel naked and alone.

Be like water, says Lao-tzu. Soft and limpid, it finds its way through, over or under any obstacle. It does not quarrel; it simply moves on.

A school bell ringing.
Children's voices drifting in
through an open window.
A temple bell across the valley,
faint.
Sheep bells high up on a
mountainside.
Heavy silver anklets.
Rain.

Do falling petals make a sound?

.Ruskin Bond.

A fanatic is never at peace.

'Rivers know this:
there is no hurry.
We shall get there some day.'
—*A.A. Milne*

'There's Music in the sighing
of a reed;
There's Music in the gushing
of a rill;
There's Music in all things,
if men had ears:
Their Earth is but an echo
of the Spheres.'
—*Lord Byron*

'With a sweet string at hand,
play a sweet song, my friend,
so we can clap and sing a song
and lose our heads in dancing.'
—*Hafiz*

'Give to me the life I love,
　Let the lave go by me,
　Give the jolly heaven above
　And the byway night me.
Bed in the bush with stars to see,
　Bread I dip in the river—
There's the life for a man like me,
　There's the life for ever.'
　　—*R. L. Stevenson*

'Silence and non-action are the
root of all things,'
says Tao. Especially on a
drowsy afternoon.

❧

'Life, exempt from public haunt,
Finds tongues in trees, books in
the running brooks,
Sermons in stones, and good
in everything.'
—*William Shakespeare*

❧

A Little Book of Serenity.

. Ruskin Bond .

.A Little Book of Serenity.

.Ruskin Bond.

How beautiful it is to do nothing,
and then rest afterwards.

— A Spanish proverb

When I open my window at night, there is almost always something to listen to: the mellow whistle of a pygmy owlet, or the sharp cry of a barking deer. Sometimes, if I'm lucky, I will see the moon coming up over the next mountain, and two distant deodars in perfect silhouette.

One melodious sound, a sweet repeated trill. Perhaps it is a little tree frog, or it may be a small green cricket. I shall never know. Th ere is so much that we shall never know. Ah, sweet mystery of life!

.Ruskin Bond.

'It is not the man who has too little that's poor, but the one who craves more.'
—*Seneca*

Stretched out on a cot under a
sky brilliant with stars.
As I close my eyes someone
brushes against the lime tree next
to me and bruises its leaves.
Th e good fresh fragrance of lime
comes to me on the night air,
and makes that moment
memorable for all time.

.Ruskin Bond.

Th e slender maidenhair fern
grows firm on a rock
While all around her the water
swirls and chatters
And then disappears in a rush
Down to the bottom of the hill.
When I am surrounded by
troubled waters, Lord,
Let me find within a rock to
cling to,
And give me the quiet patience
of the maidenhair
Who has learned to live
with the rock.

Th e sun comes out
after rain.
A lizard crawls up from a crack
in a rock.
'Small brown lizard
Basking in the sun
You too have your life to live
Your race to run.'

.Ruskin Bond.

A Little Book of Serenity.

.Ruskin Bond.

.A Little Book of Serenity.

.78.

.Ruskin Bond.

Never end your day with misunderstanding.
Sleep easy.

A kettle on the boil.
A door that creaks on its hinges.
Old sofa springs.
Familiar voices lighting
up the dark.
Ducks quacking in the rain.

Sounds that make a
house a home.

❧

'Lonely! Why should I feel
lonely? Is not our planet in the
Milky Way?'
—*Th oreau*

❧

'Finish each day and
be done with it.
You have done what you could.
Some blunders and absurdities
no doubt crept in;
forget them as soon as you can.
Tomorrow is a new day. You
shall begin it serenely
and with too high a spirit to be
encumbered with your
old nonsense.'
—*Ralph Waldo Emerson*

'When I sold my cottage and
moved on, I hung this poem on
a post in my hut:

Even a thatched hut
May change with a new owner
Into a doll's house.'
—*Matsuo Basho*

I doubt anyone in single-minded
pursuit of enlightenment
ever finds it.
A good monk would be a mild
sort of a fellow,
a bit of a sensualist,
capable of compassion for the
world, but also for himself.
He would know that it is all
right to not climb
every mountain.

'Let Nature be your teacher.

She has a world of ready wealth,
Our minds and hearts to bless—
Spontaneous wisdom
breathed by health,
Truth breathed by cheerfulness.

One impulse from a vernal wood
May teach you more of man;
Of moral evil and of good,
Th an all the sages can.'
—*William Wordsworth*

'If I were asked for the most important advice I could give, that which I considered to be the most useful to the men of our century, I should simply say: in the name of God, stop a moment, cease your work, look around you.'
—*Leo Tolstoy*

'If we have not quiet in our minds, outward comfort will do no more for us than a golden slipper on a gouty foot.'
—*John Bunyan*

A Little Book of Serenity.

.88.

.Ruskin Bond.

.89.

.A Little Book of Serenity.

.90.

.Ruskin Bond.

Preserve your sense of humour and your sense of wonder and the years pass gently.

I have lived life at my own gentle pace, and if as a result I have failed to get to the top of the mountain (or of anything else), it doesn't matter, the long walk has brought its own sweet rewards; buttercups and butterflies along the way.

As Jiddu Krishnamurti once said, 'Do you want to know what my secret is? I don't mind what happens.'

.Ruskin Bond.

October. The rains are at an end. The leeches have disappeared. The ferns are yellow, and the sunlight on the green hills is mellow and golden, like the limes on the small tree in my porch. The cold, cruel winter isn't far off, but somehow this month is longer than the others, because it is a kind month: the grass is good to be upon, the breeze is warm and gentle and pine-scented.
Everyone seems content.

'When the voices of children are
heard on the green
And laughing is heard
on the hill,
My heart is at rest within
my breast
And everything else is still.'
—*William Blake*

'Through the ample open door
of the peaceful country barn,
A sun-lit pasture field, with cattle
and horses feeding;
And haze, and vista, and the far
horizon, fading away.'
—*Walt Whitman*

Th e adventure is not in arriving,
it's in the on-the-way experience.
It's not in the expected;
it's in the surprise.
You are not choosing what you
shall see in the world,
but giving the world an even
chance to see you.

'Come, butterfly
It's late—
We've miles to go together.'
—*Matsuo Basho*

Says Ramakrishna Paramhansa:
'Travel in all the four quarters of
the earth,
yet you will find nothing
anywhere.
Whatever there is, is only here.'

We don't have to circle the world
to find beauty and fulfilment.
Most of living has to happen
in the mind.
After all, 'The world is only the
size of each man's head.'

❧

.Ruskin Bond.

When we meditate, we look
within, and hopefully there will
be something to find there.
When I look at a flower, I am
looking without contemplating
the miracle of creation.
I suppose we should do a little of
both, just for the sake of balance.

❦

'Nature does not hurry, yet
everything is accomplished.'
—*Lao Tzu*

❦

Some choose to sail around the
world in small boats.
Others remain in their own small
patch, yet see the world in a
grain of sand.

.Ruskin Bond.

Notes

A Little Book of Serenity

. Ruskin Bond .

.101.

.A Little Book of Serenity.

.Ruskin Bond.

The season of clouds,
a pitcher of wine
Roses, a rose-garden—
and you.

— Mir Taqi Mir

'Serene autumn sky,
a clear night, unsullied laughter.
Shadows fall upon a clean
footpath,
dapple, and flow;
a nectar-brook sighs.
Earth looks on in rapture,
Nature cannot keep shut
her eyes.
Th e good soothing Moon
arrives—
a nectar-drop planet-sized.'
—*Jaishankar Prasad*

'Ah vastness of pines,
murmur of waves breaking,
slow play of lights, solitary bell,
twilight falling in your eyes,
toy doll,
earth-shell, in whom the
earth sings!'
—*Pablo Neruda*

Water came dripping down from the sides of the cave, sunlight filtered through a crevice in the rock ceiling, dappling your face. A spray of water was caught by a shaft of sunlight and at intervals it reflected the colours of the rainbow.
'It is a beautiful place,' you said.
'Come then,' I said, 'let us bathe.'

Afterwards, we stretched ourselves out and allowed the sun to sink deep into our bodies.

. Ruskin Bond .

I sit against a grey rock, beneath
a sky of pristine blueness, and
think of you.
It is November and the grass
is turning brown and yellow.
Crushed, it still smells sweet.
The afternoon sun shimmers on
the oak leaves and turns them a
glittering silver.
A cricket sizzles its way through
the long grass.
The stream murmurs at the
bottom of the hill—the stream
where you and I
lingered on a golden afternoon
in May.

Better a dream of love
Than love's dream broken;
Better a look exchanged
Than love's word spoken.
Enough for me that you walk past,
A firefly flashing in the dark.

.Ruskin Bond.

But I will wait until
the sparrows bring
Shrill portents of another spring;
(And I will love you with the
same sweet pain,
If you and summer care
to visit me again.)

On an impulse I thrust a cherry seed into the soft earth and forgot all about it.

Last summer I spent a night sleeping on the grass beneath that cherry tree. I lay awake for hours, listening to the occasional tonk-tonk of nightjars and watching, through the branches overhead, the stars turning in the sky. And I felt the power of the sky and the earth, and the power of a small cherry seed…

.Ruskin Bond.

Notes

.112.

.Ruskin Bond.

.113.

.A Little Book of Serenity.

.Ruskin Bond.

Let us accept the invitation,
ever-open, from the Stillness,
taste its exquisite sweetness,
and heed its silent instruction.

— Paul Brunton

'Everything that slows us down and forces patience, everything that sets us back into the slow circles of nature, is a help. Gardening is an instrument of grace.'
—*May Sarton*

Th ose who keep good gardens are usually contented folk. Always make space for flowers, even if all you have is a window ledge.

If dandelions show a tendency to do well on the steps of the house, then that is where they shall be encouraged to grow. If a sorrel is happier on the windowsill than on the hillside, then I shall let it stay. And if the hydrangea does better in my neighbour's garden than mine, then my neighbour shall be given the hydrangea. Among flower lovers, there must be no double standards: generosity, not greed; sugar, not spite.

'Return to old watering holes for
more than water;
friends and dreams are there to
meet you.'
—*An African proverb*

It is good that others
should succeed.
Do not allow their success to cast
a shadow on your own efforts
and ruin your peace.

'If you have much,
give of your wealth
If you have little,
give of your heart.'
—*An Arabic proverb*

Make-believe is not a bad thing,
but its comfort is momentary
and only an illusion. It is like
a pain-killer; the pain returns
when the effect wears off. Th ere
can be no real contentment
unless we accept the truth and
make our peace with it.

If you owe nothing, you are rich.
Money doesn't make
people happy.
But neither does poverty.
Just enough to be
your own person,
and to lend a helping hand—
that much would be best,
I suppose.

Buddha preaches: 'Holding on to anger is like grasping a hot coal; you are the one who gets burned.'

To this I add—Before you get upset, ask yourself: does it really matter?

A Little Book of Serenity.

.Ruskin Bond.

A silent man is the best one to listen to.
— A Japanese proverb

Thank you, Lord, for silence;
The silence of the great mountains
and deserts and forests.
For the silence of the street
late at night
when the last travellers are
safely home
and the traffic is still.
For the silence in my room
in which I can hear the small
sounds outside:
a moth fluttering against the
window pane,
the drip of the dew running off
the roof,
and a field mouse rustling
through dry leaves.

.Ruskin Bond.

'He is richest who is content with the least, for content is the wealth of nature.'
—*Socrates*

The wind in the pines and deodars hums and moans, but in the chestnut it rustles and chatters and makes cheerful conversation. The horse-chestnut in full leaf is a magnificent sight.

.Ruskin Bond.

'Too lazy to be ambitious,
I let the world take care of itself.
Ten days' worth of rice
in my bag;
a bundle of twigs by
the fireplace.
Why chatter about delusion and
enlightenment?
Listening to the night rain on
my roof,
I sit comfortably, with both legs
stretched out.'
—*Taigu Ryokan*

> 'A cucumber is bitter—throw it away. There are briars in the road—turn aside from them. This is enough. Do not add, "And why were such things made in the world?"'
> —*Marcus Aurelius*

'This is thy hour O Soul, thy free
 flight into the wordless,
Away from books, away from art,
 the day erased, the lesson done,
Thee fully forth emerging, silent,
 gazing, pondering the themes
 thou lovest best.
Night, sleep, death and the stars.'
 —*Walt Whitman*

'Thus shall ye think of this
fleeting world:
A star at dawn, a bubble
in a stream,
A flash of lightning in a
summer cloud,
A flickering lamp, a phantom,
and a dream.'
—*Buddha*

A Little Book of Serenity.

. Ruskin Bond .

.137.

.138.

.Ruskin Bond.

When all wars are done, a butterfly will still be beautiful.

Th e trees watch over me
as I write.
Whenever I look up, they
remind me that they are there.
Th ey are my best critics. As long
as I am aware of their presence,
I can try to avoid the trivial and
the banal.

'Praise and esteem can feel good,
which is fine,
but don't look to them for inner
peace and lasting happiness.'
—*Allan Lokos*

Left to myself on a wall, I am soon in the throes of composing a story or poem. I do not write it down—that can be done later—I just work it out in my mind, memorize my words, so to speak, and keep them stored up for my next writing session.

Occasionally a car will stop, and someone I know will stick his head out and say, 'No work today, Mr Bond? How I envy you! Not a care in the world!'

There comes a time when almost every author asks himself what his effort and output really amounts to? We expect our work to influence people, to affect a great many readers, when in fact, its impact is infinitesimal. Those who work on a larger scale must feel discouraged by the world's indifference. That is why I am happy to give a little innocent pleasure to a handful of readers. This is a reward worth having.

.Ruskin Bond.

We cannot prevent sorrow and
pain and tragedy. And yet when
we look around us, we find
that the majority of people are
actually enjoying life! There are
so many lovely things to see,
there is so much to do, so much
fun to be had, and so many
charming and interesting people
to meet… How can my pen ever
run dry?

One evening a thief visited a
Zen master's hut only to discover
there was nothing to steal.
On his return, the master caught
him. 'You have come a long way
to visit me,' he said,
'and you should not return
empty-handed. Please take my
clothes as a gift.'
The thief was bewildered. But he
took the clothes and left.
The master sat naked, watching
the moon. 'Poor fellow,' he
mused, 'I wish I could have
given him this beautiful moon.'

. Ruskin Bond .

'Remember, sometimes not getting what you want is a wonderful stroke of luck.'
—*Dalai Lama*

To each his own particular
heaven—
heavens being as different as are
ways of life.

.Ruskin Bond.

.Ruskin Bond.

___

.A Little Book of Serenity.

.Ruskin Bond.

The sunshine beckons—
It's been a long hard winter in the hills.
But the chestnut trees are coming into new leaf,
and that's good enough for me.

'I am an old man and have
known a great many troubles,
but most of them never
happened.'
—*Mark Twain*

'Clouds come floating into my
life, no longer to carry rain or
usher storm,
but to add colour to my
sunset sky.'
Rabindranath Tagore

'Everything looms pleasant through the softening haze of time. Even the sadness that is past seems sweet. Our boyish days look very merry to us now, all nutting, hoop, and gingerbread. The snubbings and toothaches and the Latin verbs are all forgotten—the Latin verbs especially. And we fancy we were very happy when we were hobbledehoys and loved; and we wish that we could love again.'
—*Jerome K. Jerome*

'The sight-obscuring veil
thinned.
All at once, the wordless
nothingness
turned loquacious.
The sighing pine sent heady-
scented wind-messages
—though unseen.
Birds huddled in the shrubbery
called out to me in God's
own tongue.

In the far distance,
a Pahadi song.'
—*Dharamvir Bharati*

Th e little miracles of life don't happen especially for us. Sunlight will filter through leaves, dew will settle on a spider's web, birds will sing and a mountain stream bubble and chatter even when there is no one around to see or hear. All that is in our power is to be there. To be there, wherever we are.

A receptivity to the world around me—the breeze, the warmth of the old stone, the lizard on the rock, a raindrop— these and other impressions impinge upon me as I sit in that passive, benign condition that makes people smile tolerantly at me as they pass. 'Eccentric writer,' they remark to each other as they drive on, hurrying towards the pot of gold at the end of their personal rainbows. I wave to them as they rush off, and wish them luck.

.Ruskin Bond.

Our births don't come so quiet—
Most lives run riot—
But the bud opens silently,
And flower gives way to fruit.
So must we search
For the stillness within the tree,
Th e silence within the root.

I leave you, dear reader, with the
simple, profound words of
Max Ehrmann:

'Be yourself.
Especially, do not feign affection.
Neither be cynical about love;
for in the face of all aridity and
disenchantment
it is as perennial as the grass.

Take kindly the counsel of the
years,
gracefully surrendering the
things of youth.
Nurture strength of spirit to
shield you in sudden misfortune.

.Ruskin Bond.

But do not distress yourself with
dark imaginings.
Many fears are born of fatigue
and loneliness.
Beyond a wholesome discipline,
be gentle with yourself.'

Ruskin Bond is the author of numerous novellas, short-story collections and non-fiction books, many of them classics. Among them are *The Room on the Roof*, *A Flight of Pigeons*, *The Night Train at Deoli*, *Time Stops at Shamli*, *Landour Days*, *Rain in the Mountains*, *A Book of Simple Living*, *A Little Book of Happiness* and *Friends in Wild Places*. He received the Sahitya Akademi Award in 1993, the Padma Shri in 1999 and the Padma Bhushan in 2014. He lives in Landour, Mussoorie, with his extended family.

www.ingramcontent.com/pod-product-compliance
Lightning Source LLC
Chambersburg PA
CBHW061942220426
43662CB00012B/1996